Contents

Any words appearing in the text in bold, **like this**, are explained in the Glossary.

What is diabetes?

When someone has diabetes, it means that they have too much **glucose** (a kind of sugar) in their blood. This does not mean that they have been eating too many sweet foods. We all take in glucose from many different kinds of food, including pasta, bread and potatoes. As our bodies **digest** these foods, they are broken down into glucose. We all need glucose because our bodies turn it into energy. We use energy for everything we do – swimming, skateboarding and even sleeping!

In people who have diabetes, the body is unable to turn glucose into energy. Instead of being used up, the glucose builds up in their blood. This is why people with diabetes have too much glucose in their blood. It also means that they are unable to get the energy they need from the food they eat. Before they get help, many people with diabetes become very weak and tired.

Glucose is the body's main source of energy. We turn glucose from the food we eat into energy. Our bodies need energy to grow and repair themselves, and we need energy for everything we do.

What does it mean to have

Diabetes

pilsbury

Heinemann
LIBRARY

www.heinemann.co.uk/library
Visit our website to find out more information about Heinemann Library books.

To order:
☎ Phone 44 (0) 1865 888066
📄 Send a fax to 44 (0) 1865 314091
💻 Visit the Heinemann Bookshop at www.heinemann.co.uk/library to browse our
catalogue and order online.

First published in Great Britain by Heinemann Library,
Halley Court, Jordan Hill, Oxford OX2 8EJ,
a division of Reed Educational and Professional Publishing Ltd.
Heinemann is a registered trademark of Reed Educational and Professional Publishing Ltd.

OXFORD MELBOURNE AUCKLAND
JOHANNESBURG BLANTYRE GABORONE
IBADAN PORTSMOUTH (NH) USA CHICAGO

Designed by AMR
Illustrated by Art Construction and David Woodroffe
Originated by Dot Gradations
Printed in China by Wing King Tong

ISBN 0 431 13937 7 (hardback)
06 05 04 03
10 9 8 7 6 5 4 3 2

ISBN 0 431 13944 X (paperback)
07 06 05 04 03
10 9 8 7 6 5 4 3 2 1

British Library Cataloguing in Publication Data
Spilsbury, Louise
 What does it mean to have diabetes?
 1.Diabetes – Juvenile literature
 I.Title II.Diabetes
 616.4'62

Acknowledgements
The publishers would like to thank the following for permission to reproduce photographs: Bubbles: p.23;
Bubbles/Angela Hampton: pp.4, 10, 11, 17; Bubbles/Ian West: pp.14, 16; Bubbles/Roger Chester: p.25;
Format/Ulrike Preuss: pp.19, 26; Gareth Boden: pp.12, 13, 15, 22, 24, 28, 29; Life File/Nicola Sutton: p.9;
Life File/Jeff Greenberg: p.8; Life File/Jeremy Hoare: p.27; Martin Phillimore: pp.20, 21; Sally and Richard
Greenhill: p 5.

The pictures on the following pages were posed by models who do not have diabetes: pp.4, 5, 8, 9, 10, 12,
13, 14, 15, 16, 24, 25, 26, 27, 28, 29.

The following pictures were taken on commission by Trevor Clifford: pp.12–13, 15, 22, 24, 28–29

Special thanks to Myrtle and Denilka.

The publishers would also like to thank The Juvenile Diabetes Research Foundation, and Julie Johnson,
PHSE Consultant Trainer and Writer, for their help in the preparation of this book.

Cover photograph reproduced with permission of Bubbles/Angela Hampton.

Every effort has been made to contact copyright holders of any material reproduced in this book.
Any omissions will be rectified in subsequent printings if notice is given to the publishers.

People with diabetes can be treated and there is no reason why diabetes should stop anyone from doing anything or having fun.

Nowadays, people who discover they have diabetes find they can be treated successfully, and most people with diabetes lead normal lives. Doctors show people how to look after themselves, eat a healthy diet and take the medicine they need. Learning to do these things helps them to keep the amount of glucose in the blood at a normal level and get on with living their lives.

Facts about diabetes

- About 1 in every 700 schoolchildren has diabetes.
- People with diabetes are treated with medicine, eat a healthy diet and look after themselves.
- Diabetes is not **contagious**. You cannot catch it from other people.

What happens to the food we eat?

How do our bodies turn the food we eat into the energy we need to live and grow? The process is called **digestion**. As soon as you take a bite of food, your body starts to break it down into smaller pieces. These pieces travel down into the stomach where they are broken up even more. By the time the digested food reaches the small intestine, the pieces are so small they can pass through the thin walls of the intestine into the blood. Most digested food is broken down into **glucose**, a kind of sugar. The blood carries the glucose to the body's **cells**, where it is turned into energy the cells can use.

What are cells?

Our bodies are made up of millions of tiny living parts called cells. These are so small you can only see them through a microscope. Different types of cell carry out different jobs, but they all need glucose to live, grow and repair themselves.

These are the parts of the body used in digestion. After the digested food has passed into your blood, your blood carries it around your body.

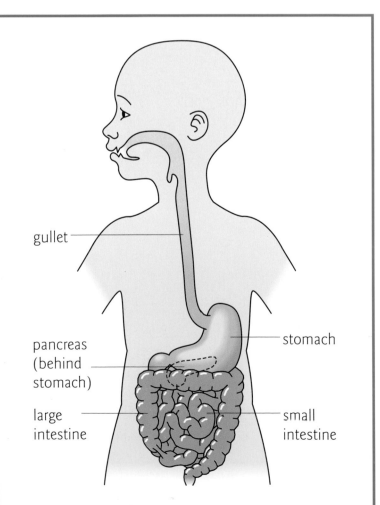

gullet

pancreas (behind stomach)

stomach

large intestine

small intestine

Getting glucose to the cells

In order that glucose can pass from the blood into the cells we all need **insulin**. Insulin travels to the cells to tell them to open up and let the glucose in. Insulin is made in the **pancreas**, a large **gland** that sits behind your stomach. As soon as extra glucose enters the blood, the pancreas sends out insulin to open the cells.

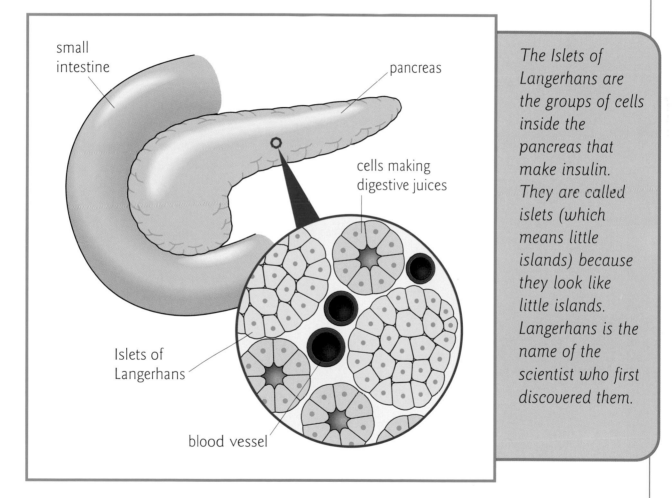

small intestine

pancreas

cells making digestive juices

Islets of Langerhans

blood vessel

The Islets of Langerhans are the groups of cells inside the pancreas that make insulin. They are called islets (which means little islands) because they look like little islands. Langerhans is the name of the scientist who first discovered them.

What happens in diabetes?

When children have diabetes, their pancreas does not work properly and is unable to make insulin. Without insulin to tell the body's cells to let the glucose in, the glucose stays in the blood. This means there is too much glucose in the blood and too little inside the body's cells.

Kinds of diabetes

There are two main kinds of diabetes. They are called
Type 1 and Type 2. If a person gets diabetes when they
are older, they are more likely to have Type 2. With this
kind some people find that their **pancreas** can still make
some **insulin**, but not as much as they need. Others find
that their pancreas makes enough insulin, but their
body cannot use it properly. People with this kind of
diabetes usually treat it by being more careful about
what they eat, taking exercise and also taking tablets
that lower their blood **glucose** levels.

Almost all children who have diabetes have Type 1.
This is the kind in which a person's pancreas makes
little or no insulin. As well as being more careful about
what they eat, they also
need to have **injections** of
insulin. If someone you
know at school has
diabetes, then this is
probably the kind they
have. Type 1 diabetes is
the kind we will be talking
about throughout this book.

*It doesn't matter how old you
are or which kind of diabetes
you have – as long as you take
care of yourself, you should be
able to do just about anything
you like.*

Before they find out what the problem is and get help, people with diabetes may feel very tired. The reason for this is that their bodies cannot use the food they eat to make energy.

How do you know if you have diabetes?

When a person feels unwell, their doctor asks them what their **symptoms** are. This means anything that feels wrong with their bodies. There are certain symptoms that immediately tell doctors a person may have diabetes. For example, when there is too much glucose (sugar) in the blood, the body gets rid of some of it in the urine (wee). This means people go to the bathroom a lot more. Because they need to drink more to replace the water they are losing, they feel thirsty all the time. Another symptom is tiredness or weakness. When the body cannot use glucose to make energy, people run out of energy and feel worn out.

If a doctor suspects diabetes, they ask whether the person has a relative with the disease. Diabetes tends to run in families, so if, say, a grandparent or uncle has it, they have a greater chance of getting it too. Finally, doctors check the person's urine or blood. If there is any glucose in the urine, or too much in the blood, it is almost certain that diabetes is the cause.

Getting better

When children first find out they have diabetes, they may have to go to hospital for a few days. Doctors there get the amount of **glucose** in their blood back to normal. Then children go to a special diabetes clinic, where everyone knows a lot about children's diabetes. A doctor decides how much **insulin** they need to take and how often they need to take it. Nurses help them with their insulin **injections** and give them lots of advice about how to cope with their diabetes at school and at home. It is also important for children to eat healthy food when they have diabetes, so they often see a dietician as well. Dieticians are people who know all about food and healthy eating.

Check-ups

Most young people with diabetes become very good at taking care of themselves, with the help of their families. Even if they are well, they still visit their clinic three or four times a year for check-ups. Doctors and nurses need to make sure that their diabetes is under control and they are keeping well.

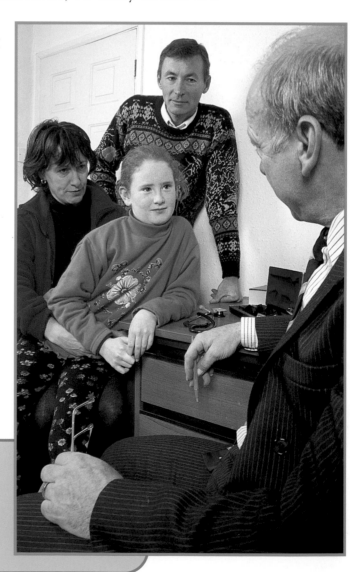

Check-ups at the diabetes clinic give people a chance to ask questions and have a chat about how they are doing.

Blood testing

People with diabetes do several **blood tests** every day to check the amount of glucose in their blood. Doing a blood test is simple and quite quick, and most people find it pretty painless. First you prick the side of a finger with a sharp needle and press the finger gently to squeeze out a drop of blood. Then you touch the blood onto a small strip of card. Some people use strips that change colour to tell them how their glucose levels are. Others may put the strip into a special little machine and read the number that comes up.

By testing a drop of blood in a blood glucose meter, you can find out how much glucose is in your blood. Children with diabetes do several blood tests a day.

It is important to write down the results of these tests and to make notes about what you ate or were doing around the time of the test. People take their notebook with them when they visit their clinic. This helps their doctor to work out how their diabetes is going, and to decide whether they need to change anything they are doing, such as the amount of insulin they take.

Meet Simon

Hi, my name is Simon and I'm ten years old. We found out that I had diabetes when I was five. My mum took me to the doctor and they did a **blood test** and my **glucose** level was really high. They sent me to the hospital straightaway.

When the doctors told her I had diabetes my mum realized I had been having the **symptoms**, but she hadn't spotted them. She thought I had been going to the bathroom a lot because I was drinking so much. As it was a really hot summer she didn't think it was strange that I was so thirsty. She thought I was tired and getting thinner because I was growing and getting taller.

The doctors explained that most kids who have diabetes seem to start off by feeling very thirsty and going to the loo a lot. You need to wee more because your body is getting rid of the extra sugar. And you get really tired because your body isn't making enough energy for you.

I don't remember much about the time I was in hospital, though I do remember my mum was crying. I felt a bit confused. I had to stay in hospital for five days so the doctors and nurses could get my blood glucose back to normal. I remember that the nurses were really nice to me and I started to feel better. While we were there, the nurses showed my mum how to give me the **injections** of **insulin** the doctor said I needed and they talked to her about me eating properly. Now I can do my own injections and I take care of my diabetes pretty much by myself.

Diabetes runs in my family. My grandad has it, so does my aunt (my mum's sister) and my cousin, Matt. My brother and sister don't have it. That annoys me sometimes. It's not that I want them to be ill, of course, but sometimes I don't think it's fair that I should have it. But I guess everyone who has diabetes feels like that sometimes. Most of the time I just get on with doing the things I enjoy, like skateboarding, playing on my computer and rock climbing.

Coping with diabetes

Young people who have diabetes become clever at doing a sort of juggling act between two things – the **insulin** they **inject** and the food they eat. Their goal is to try to keep the amount of **glucose** in their blood at a good level.

Getting your glucose levels right is a bit like riding a see-saw. Sometimes they go a little high; sometimes they go a little low. They won't always be just right. The important thing is to keep them balanced as well as you can.

It can take a while to get to learn how to balance these two things. When someone injects insulin, the insulin heads off to tell his or her **cells** to open up and get ready to take in glucose. After injecting, they have to make sure there is enough glucose in their blood for the insulin to work on. That means eating enough of the right kinds of food. Most people with diabetes do **blood tests** every day to check that they are getting the balance right.

When a 'hypo' happens

It is tricky to get the balance right all the time. Sometimes people with diabetes feel ill because there is not enough glucose in their body. This is called 'hypoglycaemia' (said hypoe-glyceemeea). It can happen when the insulin they have injected does not have enough food (glucose) to work on. It may make them feel tired, dizzy, sweaty or tearful. Most people know exactly what to do if they have a '**hypo**'. If someone in your class has diabetes, you might like to know how to help.

- As soon as someone has a hypo, they should stop what they are doing.

- Tell the teacher straightaway. Put your hand up and interrupt the lesson if you have to.

- The person should have something sugary to eat or drink. Most people with diabetes always carry sweet snacks with them.

- After they have eaten or drunk something sugary, they need to have something more solid, like sandwiches and a glass of milk.

- Next they should sit down for 15 minutes or so. When they feel better, they can get back to whatever they were doing before.

If you have diabetes, it is a good idea to keep a sugary snack or sweet drink handy at all times, just in case.

15

Injecting insulin

All children with diabetes need to have **injections** of **insulin**. An injection puts the insulin straight into the blood where it is needed. Insulin cannot be taken like a syrupy medicine on a spoon because the **digestive juices** in the stomach would destroy it before it could get into the blood.

Children may have two, three or four injections of insulin a day. Children who have two usually have one before their breakfast and one before their evening meal. Children who need a third or even fourth injection, probably have to have one before lunch and after school.

If you have diabetes, you always give yourself an insulin injection before you eat a main meal. That way it is already in your blood waiting to work when glucose from your food arrives.

Inject before you eat!

Children with diabetes should always have an insulin injection just before a meal like breakfast or dinner. Foods like pasta, potatoes, bread and cereals put **glucose** into your blood, so if you have diabetes, you need to make sure your body has a supply of insulin before you eat.

How is it done?

The thought of giving themselves an injection bothers a lot of people. Some young people ask someone else, such as a parent, to give them their insulin. Others prefer to do it themselves. This lets them be more independent. They can stay overnight at a friend's house or go away on a school trip because they can take care of themselves. Many say that it feels good to take responsibility for their diabetes and their own bodies.

Nurses teach people how to give themselves an injection. There are lots of places on your body where you can inject insulin, including the tops of your arms, your stomach, thighs and bottom. It helps the injection to work better if you don't inject in the same part of your body every time.

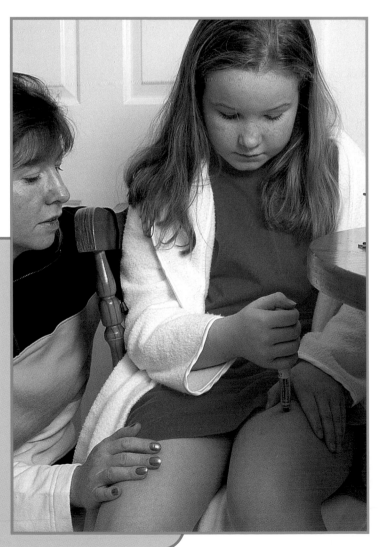

*Lots of people find **pen injectors** simple to use. The insulin comes in little tubes, rather like the ones you use in cartridge ink pens. You pop one of these into the 'pen', press it against your skin and the pen injector does the rest.*

Eat well!

The rules for healthy eating are the same whether or not you have diabetes. People with diabetes do not have to eat anything special. We should all eat a range of different foods in order to stay healthy.

We can divide the foods we eat into five different groups, as you can see in the picture on this page. The idea is that the biggest group, the **carbohydrates**, should be our main source of energy. We should eat some carbohydrates, such as pasta, cereals or potatoes, at every meal. We should also try to eat fresh fruit and vegetables at every meal, as these keep us fit and well. **Proteins** like meat, fish, eggs and beans help us grow, but we should not eat large amounts of these. Dairy products, such as milk and cheese, keep our bones and teeth strong, although we do not need to eat very much of these. We should all save sweet and fatty foods, like chocolate and chips, for treats only and not eat them every day.

*Different kinds of foods help our bodies in different ways. If you have diabetes, eating plenty of carbohydrates will help you keep your **glucose** levels under control.*

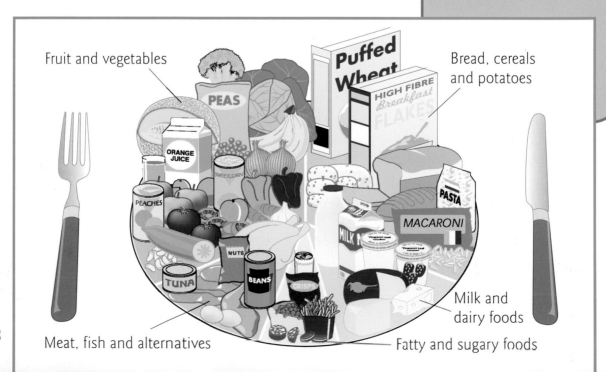

Fruit and vegetables

Bread, cereals and potatoes

PEAS

Puffed Wheat

HIGH FIBRE Breakfast FLAKES

ORANGE JUICE

SWEETCORN

PASTA

MACARONI

PEACHES

MILK

NUTS

TUNA

BEANS

CRISPS

Milk and dairy foods

Meat, fish and alternatives

Fatty and sugary foods

Lots of young people with diabetes save sweet treats for when they need a boost of energy for sport or dancing.

The time is right!

The only real difference for people who have diabetes is that they should try to eat their meals at the same time each day. They also need to eat snacks in the morning, in the afternoon and at bedtime, even if they don't really feel hungry. The **insulin** they inject goes on working all day so they need to eat a steady supply of food to make sure there is enough glucose in their blood for it to work on. People with diabetes need a snack at bedtime because even when we are asleep our bodies are using up energy. Our **cells** are still at work – growing, repairing themselves and keeping us alive.

'Fast' food?

People with diabetes try not to eat a lot of chocolate, fizzy drinks and sweets because these foods can put too much glucose into the blood too quickly. However, sweet foods are useful once in a while, when people with diabetes need to get some glucose fast, say before doing something energetic or if they have a '**hypo**'.

Meet Myrtle and Denika

Hello. My name is Myrtle and I'm Denika's mum. Denika is eight years old now and she has had diabetes since just before her third birthday.

Denika has two **injections** of **insulin** a day, one before breakfast and one before our evening meal. She gives herself the injections with a **pen injector**. She also does her own **blood tests**. She writes down the test result and what she has been eating in a notebook. This helps us understand any ups and downs in the level of glucose in her blood, say if she has had a piece of birthday cake on the way home from school. Denika also takes her blood test meter to school with her. If she feels a bit low, she goes out of class and does a test. When she needs extra sugar she goes to the office, where we keep **glucose tablets** she can use.

We often go to meetings and events with other children who have diabetes. It's nice for Denika to know she is not the only child to have diabetes. She also makes new friends and has a lot of fun during the holidays and family days that the Diabetes Parents' Group organize.

My name is Denika. I have diabetes, but it doesn't stop me doing the things I want to do. I really like swimming, skipping and roller-skating. I also like riding my bike for a long time. There is a park near my home that we sometimes go to. I'm good at swimming as well. At school I quite like doing drama and gym. I like language and maths lessons, too, as I am good at them.

I go to a club for children who have diabetes. They give us parties and discos and presents at Christmas. I like dancing. I've made some friends at the club and they like dancing, too.

I would say to children who don't have diabetes that you can't get it unless you are born with it. You can't catch diabetes from someone else. Also, children and grown-ups who have diabetes can't eat a lot of sweet things unless they are doing a lot of exercise or they are having a **hypo**.

Living with diabetes

If you have diabetes, it is something you have to live with and deal with every day, whatever else is going on in your life. Once you have learned how to give yourself **injections**, and how to do **blood tests** and work out what they mean, you have to keep on doing these things every day. For most people, managing their diabetes gradually becomes just a way of life, but it is not always easy.

Just in case

Most people who have diabetes are good at keeping it under control and feel perfectly fine most of the time. Just in case they have a '**hypo**' while they are out of school or away from home, some people choose to wear an identity card, bracelet or necklace. This has a special symbol on the front that is recognized all over the world. It tells people that you have a special medical **condition**. On the back your condition, membership number and a telephone number are listed. Doctors can ring the number and find out all your medical information and needs from a computer.

Doctors and nurses across the world will recognize the symbols on these chains and bracelets.

Trips for groups of people who have diabetes are like any other activity holiday. People play games, learn new sports and make new friends – and probably come back worn out after too many late nights!

Getting together

Some young people who have diabetes like to meet other people who have diabetes. It is good to know you are not the only one who has to have **injections** and **blood tests** every day. In many countries there are organizations especially for young people with diabetes. At meetings people get the chance to talk about their diabetes and share information or pass on useful advice. Some groups arrange activity holidays run by people who have a lot of experience with diabetes. They are on hand to offer help if you need it. As well as being good fun, these trips also give you a chance to learn something new about your diabetes and to talk to other people about it.

At school

School life for people with diabetes is much the same as it is for anyone else. The only real difference is that children with diabetes may need to give themselves a **blood test** or an **injection** at school, and they also need to be careful to eat on time and to have regular snacks. As soon as someone finds out that they have diabetes, they meet with their teacher to talk about how they would like to manage things at school. If necessary, they decide where to keep their **insulin** and test equipment and where to do injections.

Some children like their teacher or the school nurse to explain to the rest of the class what it means to have diabetes. This helps other people understand why they may have to have a snack in the afternoon or why they might sometimes feel unwell. It is also a good chance to explain to others that having diabetes does not stop you doing anything, or make you different in any way.

Most children with diabetes try to have their snacks at break time. If the class does not usually have an afternoon break, they may need to eat a snack in class.

Exercise is good for you!

It is important for all of us to get out there and exercise our bodies. Doing some kind of sport, either in school or out of it, is a great way to stay healthy and fit and to feel good about yourself.

The only thing you need to be aware of if you have diabetes is your blood **glucose** level. Doing any kind of exercise makes the amount of glucose in your blood drop. The reason is that your body uses up more glucose than usual to make the extra energy you need. If you have diabetes, you should boost your glucose levels with a snack, like a banana or cake, before you exercise. If you are playing an energetic game like football or basketball, it is a good idea to have some fruit juice at half time as well. Most people also keep an extra snack or some **glucose tablets** nearby, in case the game goes on a bit longer than they expected.

As long as they take care of their glucose levels there is really nothing to stop someone with diabetes scoring the winning goal – except the opposition!

At home

Sometimes brothers and sisters of people who have diabetes say they feel jealous of all the attention the person with diabetes gets from their parents. This is often worse just after the diabetes has been discovered. Parents may have to spend time at the hospital with the child who has diabetes, for example learning about how to give **injections**. This can make the rest of the family feel left out. On the other hand, the child with diabetes may feel angry that they have diabetes when their brothers and sisters don't. They may feel jealous that they cannot just please themselves like their brothers and sisters do, but always have to remember to do tests and injections and take snacks with them wherever they go.

It is perfectly normal for brothers and sisters to argue or to feel jealous of each other sometimes. Most families find that life settles down when the diabetes has become a part of everyday life.

Most people who have a brother or sister who has diabetes say they don't even think about it most of the time. There are lots of other things they would rather be doing together.

If you have diabetes you need to stick to your usual routines for doing injections or blood tests when you go on holiday. Apart from that, the only thing to remember is to have lots of fun!

Family holidays

Family holidays are a great chance to get away from the usual chores and have fun. If you have diabetes you just need to make sure that the change in routine does not interfere with your diabetes treatment. It is a good idea for us all to make a list before we start packing, so we don't forget anything. If you have diabetes the first things on that list should be your **insulin**, **pen injector** or **syringe** and **blood testing** equipment. Take all the insulin you will need for the whole holiday, just in case you cannot get hold of any more.

For the journey, don't forget to take a packed lunch and a supply of snacks and **glucose tablets**. This is important even if you are planning to stop for lunch somewhere, just in case there are any hold-ups. Biscuits, fruit and cakes are ideal and you can pop them in a pocket so they are close by if you need them.

Meet Hattie

Hello. My name is Harriet, but I like to be called Hattie. I'm nine now and I've had diabetes since I was four. I have a mum and dad, two brothers and a pet dog called Spice. I like gymnastics, dancing, running, swimming, reading and playing with my two best friends, Isabel and Lottie. Before doing something like gym club I have to eat a snack like a chocolate bar to make sure there is enough **glucose** in my blood. Our gym teacher trains us pretty hard so I always burn up lots of energy at gym. I keep other food and my **glucose tablets** handy, just in case.

I'm the only one in my family who has diabetes. Sometimes my two brothers get fed up because they say I get all the attention. Like at dinnertime, mum usually gives me my food first because once I have had my **injection** of **insulin** I need to have something to eat to make sure I've got enough glucose inside me. I think they understand really. They always look out for me at school, and check that I've eaten my snack at break time.

I do my own insulin injections – two at home and one in school at lunchtime. I use a **pen injector** and I check my blood glucose with a little machine. I don't mind doing the injections but I get fed up with doing the **blood tests** because my fingers sometimes get sore. Still, I'm the only one in my school who's got diabetes so my friends are really impressed that I can do my injections and tests by myself. In fact my teacher gave my whole class a talk about diabetes. She did it after someone was complaining that I was the only one who was allowed to have a snack in class.

Sometimes when I tell other people I've got diabetes, they look at me as if they feel sorry for me. I wish they wouldn't. I don't mind having diabetes at all. Well, most of the time I don't. Because I've got diabetes I take care of myself. I know what I need to eat to stay healthy and I like doing lots of exercise. It feels good to be fit and well. I don't let my diabetes slow me down at all.

Glossary

blood tests when a tiny sample of blood is taken and tested. People who have diabetes check the amount of glucose in their blood by testing a drop of blood from a finger.

carbohydrates foods such as bread, potatoes, rice, pasta and cereals. Carbohydrates give us energy because the body breaks them down into sugars.

cells all living things are made up of millions of tiny parts called cells. Different parts of the body are made up of groups of millions of cells.

condition word used to describe an illness or disease that a person has for a long time, perhaps for all their life.

contagious a contagious disease can be passed on by coughing, touching or other kinds of contact. Diabetes is not contagious.

digest/digestion way in which our bodies break down the food we eat. Some of it is turned into energy and the rest is passed out of our bodies as waste.

digestive juices stomach juices that help you digest food

gland body part which has a particular job to do. The pancreas is a gland.

glucose kind of sugar. Most of the food we eat is broken down into glucose when we digest it.

glucose tablets special tablets that look a bit like sweets and contain lots of glucose

hypo short for hypoglycaemia (you say 'hypoe-glyceemeea'). This happens when there are lower than normal levels of blood glucose in a person with diabetes. It can make them feel dizzy, shaky and their vision may be blurred. They may eventually lose consciousness.

injection way of taking medicine. This is usually done with a fine needle, which is inserted under the skin. The medicine is then taken into the bloodstream.

insulin chemical made by a part of your body called the pancreas. Insulin allows the cells in your body to use food.

pancreas gland found at the back of our stomachs. It makes insulin and some other chemicals our bodies use to help them digest food.

pen injector people use this to inject insulin. It looks like a pen.

proteins foods that give us the energy we need to grow, such as meat, fish, eggs and beans

symptom something your body feels that tells you something is wrong. Diabetes symptoms include being thirsty, needing to pass water a lot, feeling tired and losing weight.

syringe small tube with a needle at one end, which is used to inject medicines through the skin and into a person's body.

Helpful books and addresses

BOOKS

Living with Diabetes, Jenny Bryan, Wayland Publishers, 1998

Living with Diabetes, Barbara Taylor, Franklin Watts, 1989

Body Systems: Eating and Digestion, Anita Ganeri, Heinemann Library, 1997.

WEBSITES

www.castleweb.com.diabetes has a special site for young people, where they can share stories and make friends.

www.diabetes.com/site is an American site that has lots of information and useful links, and a special section for young people.

www.childrenwithdiabetes.com

ORGANIZATIONS

Juvenile Diabetes Research Foundation (UK)
25 Gosfield Street
London W1W 6EB
Telephone: 0207 436 3112
Website: www.jdrf.org.uk

Diabetes UK (formerly the British Diabetic Association) works with and supports people who have diabetes. It has a club and magazines for young people.
10 Queen Street
London WIM OBD.
Telephone: 0207 323 1531
Website: www.diabetes.org.uk

IN AUSTRALIA

International Diabetes Institute Australia
260 Kooyong Road
Caulfield VIC 3162
Telephone: 03 9258 5000
Fax: 03 9258 5090
Website: www.diabetes.com.au

Juvenile Diabetes Research Foundation (Australia)
National Office
Level 1
48 Atchison Street
St Leonards NSW 2065
Tel: 02 9966 0400
Fax: 02 9966 0172
Website: www.jdrf.org.au

Diabetes Australia
National Office
Churchill House
1st Floor
218 Northbourne Avenue
Braddon ACT 2612
Tel: 02 6230 1155
Fax: 02 6230 1551
E-mail: mail@diabetesaustralia.com.au

Index